FRENCH AND INDIAN

A History From Beginning to End

Copyright © 2017 by Hourly History

Table of Contents

Introduction

With the conclusion of the Seven Years' War in 1763, a great dispute between two European powers had apparently been resolved once and for all. France's dominance in North America was forever ended, as Britain came to control not merely the eastern coast of America but all of the land between the Atlantic Ocean and the Appalachian Mountains, including the coveted Ohio Valley as well the great expanse of Canada.

Yet the French and Indian War, as the dispute is commonly called in America, is rarely granted pride of place in American history books. Seen principally as one step in the inexorable march to American independence, this view betrays the complexity of the imperial realities of the eighteenth century. For most of the war, France clearly held the upper hand, winning victory after victory, with England struggling to maintain control of its frontier. The conflict beginning in the wilderness of America ultimately became a global war, with blood spilled on battlefields across Europe, in the islands of the Caribbean, even in the far-flung domains of India and the Philippines. Further, though Great Britain emerged the victor, France retained control not only of the port of New Orleans but of an incomprehensibly large tract of land from the Mississippi River to the Rocky Mountains known as "Louisiana."

Also, the typical examination of the French and Indian War betrays the name given to the conflict. While the fighting was focused on disputed territories claimed by both the French and British crowns, there were numerous nations of Indians whose lands were also at stake. These Indian tribes had little choice but to ally themselves with one power or the other, though they too were constantly striving to secure their own best interests in the outcome of the war. On more than one occasion, it was the presence of

Indian allies - or the lack of such - that tipped the balance of power in battle.

Moreover, history books are also prone to oversimplify the relationship of the British crown with his American colonial subjects. In the century or more since the earliest British colonies were formed, generations of white settlers had indeed developed their own American identity. However, while there were always the usual bureaucratic difficulties and conflicts of interest in the interaction of colonial governments with Parliament, there remained no question of the colonists' allegiance to king and country. Indeed, many colonists were gripped with patriotic fervor over the emergence of the British Empire as the dominant world power by the war's end. They foresaw a mighty kingdom in which the British crown presided over strong and prosperous people the world over. Yet even as the colonists sought to assert themselves as loyal and valuable partners in Great Britain's imperial supremacy, the seeds of revolution were sown in this nationalistic soil. Within a generation, and as a direct result of policies established during the French and Indian war, Americans would fight to free themselves from the empire they helped establish.

As the conflict between the French and the British was kindled in the Ohio Valley in 1753, few could have foreseen the direction it would take, or the scope it would encompass. The stakes were high, and the prize was great. The victor of the French and Indian War would determine the future of North America. The fate of the continent hung in the balance.

Chapter One

Imperial Appetites

"The flames of war, once kindled, often spread far and wide, and the mischief is infinite."

—Benjamin Franklin, 1760

Beginning with Christopher Columbus' legendary journey across the Atlantic, the European nations were quickly embroiled in a New World race for land, gold, and power. Certainly, the contest had begun centuries earlier, as the various people groups throughout Europe consolidated themselves into powerful nation-states no longer ruled by a single emperor. The key to security, these nations understood, lay in power - and the key to power was wealth in all its many forms: land, resources, and especially gold.

The discovery of vast new lands to the west opened up the possibility of unfathomable riches, and those monarchs who could devote the resources to exploration wasted no time in sending their own contingents of intrepid pioneers to lay claim to as much of the wealth as they could. Thus the 16th and 17th centuries saw the continents of the western hemisphere infiltrated and subdued under Dutch, Portuguese, Spanish, French, and English flags. In this way the flow of people, goods, and wealth from the New World to the Old began, intensifying the never-ending power struggles among the established European nations.

By the dawn of the 18th century, the North American continent had been largely subdued by France. From their stronghold at Quebec, they maintained control of the St. Lawrence River, building forts and establishing trade routes throughout the Great Lakes region all the way down the Mississippi River to the Gulf of Mexico. With the establishment of New Orleans in 1718, the domain of King Louis XV dwarfed the meager settlements of the English along the eastern coast of America. The French crown viewed New France primarily as an economic venture, one in which a handful of fur trappers and merchants were to exploit the wealth of the continent in order to enrich the old country. Settlement, therefore, was limited, and the number of French colonists remained small compared to the populations rapidly filling the English territories.

England was slower than other nations to join the race for supremacy in the New World. Their first attempt at settlement, the lost colony of Roanoke, had ended in failure by 1590. While the oldest surviving English settlement founded at Jamestown in 1607 attracted many who hoped to cash in on the economic promise of the New World, America was attractive to other English settlers for religious reasons. Many Puritans who were dissatisfied with the Church of England sailed for the New World in order to practice Christianity as they saw fit. These first pilgrims established the Plymouth Colony in 1620 and set a precedent for migration to America not just for capital-seeking adventurers but for also for families. The population was able to grow, then, not merely by immigration, but by procreation. As England established colonies up and down the eastern coast throughout the 17th century, the numbers of white inhabitants, along with the importation of black slaves, increased the non-native population to over a million by the mid-18th century. While New France dwarfed the English lands in territory, the English colonies towered over the French in population. This disparity would inevitably lead to conflict.

Dispersed throughout the North American continent, and forced to come to terms with the relentless flood of white settlers into their lands, were the many peoples native to the American continent. Dubbed "Indians" by Columbus, who initially believed he had landed in India, these Native Americans were themselves powerful and in many ways sophisticated in using the political conflicts of the European nations to their immediate advantage. Sadly, however, the weapon they had no ability to fight was the diseases that the European explorers and settlers unintentionally brought with them. Measles, chicken pox, smallpox, and other infectious diseases rampaged throughout the Native American communities with inexorable force, as the Indians had no immunity to them. The result was a massive decrease in native population; some scholars estimate up to 90% of North American Indians eventually succumbed to these diseases.

The remaining Indians then were faced with the dilemma of not only maintaining their territory but also of sustaining their populations. Most tribes resorted to raiding and captive-taking from other tribes and from the white settlements, a practice involving the execution or enslavement of the captured adult men and the assimilation of the women and children. The tribes that were the most successful at this were those with access to European weapons: swords and guns. Therefore Native Americans found that their best interest lay in persistent contact and friendly trade with the very Europeans who had brought the dreaded diseases among them in the first place. In an ironic twist of history, the success of the French and English enterprises in the New World rested largely on their unintentional introduction of disease into the indigenous peoples, and on the resulting wars that further weakened the native populations. Still, many of the Indian tribes found ways to survive and benefit from close relationships with the European traders and settlers in the midst of their rapidly changing political and economic landscape.

Perhaps these disparate groups could have learned to share the vast expanse and the wealth of the North American continent, coexisting by means of diplomacy and mutually beneficial trade, but it was not to be. As wars raged in Europe throughout the early 18th century, the military presences in the colonial outposts took advantage of the hostilities to expand their own territory. Hence the War of Spanish succession (1702-1713), which pitted France and Spain against England and much of the old Holy Roman Empire, was known in the colonies as Queen Anne's War. This continental conflict saw the French's Indian allies burn the town of Deerfield, Massachusetts, to the ground, while English settlers tried and failed to capture Quebec to the north and the Spanish settlement of Saint Augustine to the south. The war ended with the Treaty of Utrecht in 1713, which sought to restore the balance of power in North America but did little to curb the violence frequently erupting along the colonial frontiers. When the War of Austrian Succession began thirty years later, France and England again found themselves on opposite sides of the conflict, and so the governor of Massachusetts led an improbable campaign to besiege the French fortress of Louisbourg at the mouth of the St. Lawrence River. Improbable though it was, the campaign was successful; the rather unprofessional New Englanders took control of the fort once thought to have been impenetrable. This was the greatest English success of the conflict, known among colonists as King George's War, though Louisbourg was returned to the French when peace was declared in 1748 with the Treaty of Aix-la-Chapelle.

The peace was uneasy at best. Not only were the colonies angered by Parliament's agreement to return Louisbourg to French control, they felt increasingly threatened by what they saw as French and Indian cooperation along their frontiers to assert control of the Ohio Valley. Meanwhile, in Europe, the peace treaty effectively restored the major European powers to the territories they held before the war, which satisfied none of the nations' leaders. The treaty amounted to little more than a ceasefire, with hostilities to be resumed upon the next provocation.

Inevitably, the native peoples were drawn into the larger dynamic of conflict among the European powers they knew little about. As the wars on the continent spilled over into the New World, the various Indian tribes tried their hand at alliances with both France and England, yet the famed Iroquois League - a confederation of five Indian nations including the Mohawk, Oneida, Onondaga, Cayuga, and Seneca tribes ranging throughout upstate New York - rose to prominence not only in their successful raiding and captive-taking from other Indian tribes but also by securing a position of neutrality in the French-English conflicts. The Iroquois served as a powerful counter-balance of stability during the turmoil of the continuing wars, using the wide Ohio Valley as a buffer between the two colonial powers and holding sway over the various other tribes who lived there.

The Ohio Valley is a vast territory of land west of the Appalachian Mountains that drains into the Ohio River, which the French called "Belle Riviere," or "beautiful river." The land of the valley is fertile and rich, and the French forts were many miles away to the west, a fact not lost on the English colonial governments situated on the east coast. When the colonial charters were originally granted by the British crown, they included language that claimed the lands to the west "indefinitely" or from "sea to sea," so colonists felt no compunction about pushing the boundaries of their lands into the Ohio country. Beginning in 1750, members of the Ohio Company of Virginia sent land surveyor Christopher Gist into the Ohio Valley to explore the land and to establish trading contacts with local Indians. Similarly, an Irish trader from Pennsylvania, George Croghan, had established trading posts as far as west as modern-day Cleveland. These settlers were in fierce competition not only with the French but with one another, and they won Indian allies by providing them with cheap goods and generous gifts. In 1752, New France was appointed a new governor, the Marquis Duquesne, who saw these British incursions into the Ohio Valley as direct defiance of French sovereignty. Duquesne's solution was to assert French control militarily by building a series of forts along the Ohio. The most strategic of these forts was named for himself, Fort Duquesne, and was located where the Ohio River meets the Allegheny and Monongahela Rivers. This increased French military presence sent a foreboding message to the British colonies. The uneasy peace was rapidly becoming untenable.

Chapter Two

Sparks Ignite

"They told me, that it was their absolute design to take possession of the Ohio, and, by God, they would do it."

—Major George Washington, 1754

Robert Dinwiddie, Virginia's lieutenant governor, was determined to protect what he believed were the rightful boundaries of the British Empire. He asked for and received authorization to remove the French, by force if necessary, from their forts and then to erect British fortifications on the site. Although he had authorization, he did not have the necessary funds. While waiting for the money to be allocated, Dinwiddie sent a young Major George Washington as an emissary to insist that the French leave their newly-constructed forts and to secure Indian support for Virginia's land claims. Accordingly, Washington set out from Williamsburg, VA, in October of 1753, bound for Fort le Boeuf.

Washington secured the aid of the experienced Ohio Valley explorer Christopher Gist, who guided Washington across the Allegheny River to a trading post at a place called Logstown. There Washington met with Tanaghrisson, the Iroquois-appointed leader of the Ohio Indian tribes, also known as the Half King, who gave assurances of their support for the British-proposed defenses. He also accompanied Washington on his journey.

The journey to Fort le Boeuf was significant for two reasons. First, this expedition was the first time George Washington laid eyes on the Ohio Valley. Washington had a particular interest in land speculation, not least because his half-brother Lawrence had been one of the original shareholders in the Ohio Company. On this journey, Washington saw for himself the lay of the land and the strategic points within it. After surveying the site where the Ohio Company intended to build their fort, Washington suggested an alternative: "A fort at the forks [of the Ohio River, where the three rivers meet] would be equally well situated on [the] Ohio and have the entire command of [the] Monongahela." In the coming year, the Virginia legislature would take Washington's suggestion to heart.

The second reason Washington's journey was significant was that, upon presenting the French Captain Jacques Legardeur de Saint-Pierre with the letter from Governor Dinwiddie demanding the French abandon their forts, the French captain politely refused. Saint Pierre claimed he did not have the authority to withdraw his men from the fort, but would forward the message on to Governor Duquesne. Washington then returned to Williamsburg in January of 1754 to report the result of his journey to Dinwiddie. Despite its rather anti-climactic ending, the French insistence on maintaining their presence in the Ohio Valley made Washington's expedition a noteworthy one, for it left Dinwiddie no recourse but "to enforce by arms" the removal of the French from what England claimed to be "His Majesty's dominions."

Dinwiddie set about gathering the necessary funds and men to build a new garrison, Fort Prince George, at the place Washington had suggested at the forks of the Ohio River. He also promoted Washington to Lieutenant-Colonel and tasked him with leading a new Virginia regiment that would defend the fort. In April of 1754, Washington marched a small number of troops to Wills Creek, Virginia. There he intended to train his men while waiting for an additional company of troops and supplies under the command of Colonel Joshua Frye before moving on to Fort Prince George, but after just a few days at Wills Creek, word came to Washington that the French, a company of 500 strong, were canoeing down the Allegheny, presumably for the purpose of constructing their own fort at the same place. The site would become home to the French Fort Duquesne.

Despite his far inferior numbers, Washington still intended to fulfill his orders. Continuing the march, Washington and his men made camp that spring at a place called Great Meadows. There they waited for reinforcements of troops and supplies. On May 27, having received word that French soldiers were in the area, Washington feared an attack. After a long march to join up with his Iroquois ally Tanaghrisson, the Half King then led Washington and his men to the French camp. The soldiers, unaware of the English presence, were preparing their breakfast as Washington and Tanaghrisson arrayed their men around them.

It is unclear how the shooting began on the morning of May 28. Both sides maintained the first musket shots were not their own. Nonetheless, Washington had the advantage, and the French soon called for a ceasefire. In the ensuing discussion, the wounded French commander, Joseph Coulon de Villiers de Jumonville, explained his mission: to order the Virginian troops to evacuate the Ohio Valley, the rightful possession of the King of France. Before Washington could respond, Tanaghrisson took it upon himself to kill Jumonville with a single blow from his hatchet. The Half King's warriors present then began killing the rest of the French wounded while Washington struggled to end the bloodshed. In the end, 21 prisoners were taken, though one of the French soldiers escaped, returning to Fort Duquesne.

The event was, by all accounts, a disaster; the situation would get much worse for Washington. He retreated to Great Meadows, still hoping for the arrival of Colonel Frye with more troops and supplies. In the meantime, he ordered his men to erect a small stockade within their camp, which was aptly named Fort Necessity. On June 3, word arrived that Colonel Frye was dead from a fall off his horse and that Dinwiddie had promoted Washington to Colonel. Washington alone was in command.

On July 3, a company of 700 soldiers and 350 Indians arrived from Fort Duquesne and attacked Washington at Fort Necessity. There was little Washington and his men could do to defend themselves, given that they had no cover from a driving rain that was filling the trenches around Fort Necessity, soaking their powder. The next day, July 4, 1754, Washington surrendered to the French commander, Captain Louis Coulon de Villiers. The terms of surrender allowed for Washington and his men to retain "the honors of war," provided that Washington sign articles of capitulation which were, unfortunately, written in French. The Virginian colonel knew no French and was unaware that the document contained an admission that he was responsible for the assassination of Ensign Jumonville. In effect, Washington had professed himself to be guilty of an act of war. Though war would not be officially declared by France until 1756, this inauspicious beginning for Colonel Washington not only ensured France's hold on the Ohio Valley but effectively put the wheels of the French and Indian war into motion.

Chapter Three

Rumours of War

"The French seem to have advanced further towards making themselves masters of this continent within these last five or six years than they have done ever since the first beginning of their settlements upon it."

—William Shirley, Governor of Massachusetts, 1754

After Washington's defeat at Fort Necessity, the British government sought to stave off war by increasing numbers of troops in America - both British regular soldiers and colonial militia - and embarking on a tour de force in which they would seize not only Fort Duquesne on the Ohio River but Fort Niagara on Lake Ontario and Fort Frederick (also known as Crown Point) on Lake Champlain. Their hope was to secure these critical locations on the Canadian frontier, stunning and weakening France's colonial forces before the French crown could respond by sending reinforcements. By striking hard first, England could protect her future presence in the Ohio Valley while still avoiding an all-out war with France.

This could not be done without the help of the mighty Iroquois League. The Indian confederacy, now composed of six nations since the admission of the Tuscaroras in 1726, had spent the greater part of the 18th century actively engaged in a kind of dual diplomacy with France and England that confounded the two colonial powers' attempts at supremacy. Each nation needed the friendship of the Iroquois in order for their imperial experiments to succeed, and the

Indians took full advantage of their officially neutral status to enrich themselves at colonial expense. This enrichment came primarily through the old practice of "gift-giving," in which French and English settlers would present Indian tribes with gifts of food, clothing, alcohol, weapons, and manufactured goods as a means of ensuring the tribe's allegiance, or, barring that, at least a measure of non-interference in their colonial endeavors. Though the Iroquois did routinely interfere with French and English affairs, their appearance of neutrality guaranteed the continued flow of gifts from both governments. This friendly relationship with England had been established in the 1690s and was known as the Covenant Chain.

The British government had initiated a meeting between colonial and Iroquois representatives to take place in Albany, New York, in June 1754. At the meeting, the Iroquois made demands regarding land, citing the obvious fact that settlers from Pennsylvania and Virginia were just as much a threat to their sovereignty as the French. The negotiations accomplished little of substance, but in the end, the Iroquois left the Albany conference with thirty wagons loaded with presents.

Yet another matter of significance was swirling in conversation amongst the colonial delegates to the Albany conference. One of the Pennsylvania delegates was the deputy postmaster general for North America, Benjamin Franklin, who had long been an advocate of some sort of colonial union. In May of 1754, he published what is widely considered to be America's first political cartoon on the subject of union; the drawing depicted a snake cut into many pieces, with each piece representing one of the colonies, along with the caption, "Join or Die." Franklin's idea was that the colonies, which were currently, governed by separate legislative bodies each reporting independently to the Crown, needed some form of organization with authority to address the mutual concerns of the colonies, particularly defense. Franklin, therefore, proposed the Albany Plan of Union, a document which called for the creation of a grand council elected by the colonial legislatures and chaired by a president-general to be appointed by the king. The grand council would have authority to levy taxes, to regulate Indian relations, and to provide for the colonies' defense. Though the colonial delegations approved the plan, none of the colonies' legislatures bothered to ratify it. Still, many of the ideas put forth in the Albany Plan of Union in 1754 would surface again in the Constitutional Convention of the young United States.

By the spring of 1755, England had dispatched a new military commander in chief of North America, Major General Edward Braddock, to put its multi-pronged campaign into motion. Braddock was an abrasive man. He succeeded in alienating many of the colonial governors almost immediately upon his arrival by calling a meeting in Alexandria, Virginia, and then proceeding to dictate to them the outline of the proposed campaign, rather than asking for their assistance. In an example of his arrogance, Braddock utterly disregarded a plan of Fort Duquesne that had been smuggled out and offered to him by a Mohawk Indian named Moses the Song. Rather, he was convinced he needed no Indian help to dislodge the French from their stronghold. Not coincidentally, the Indians did not offer Braddock any more.

Thanks to a robust network of spies, the French king was well aware of England's plans to raid their forts in 1755. He countered accordingly by sending 3,000 professional soldiers to Canada under the command of military leader Baron Ludwig August Dieskau. New France came under the leadership of a new governor as well, Pierre Francois de Rigaud de Vaudreuil. The English government attempted to prevent the flow of men and supplies into New France by means of a naval blockade, which was wholly unsuccessful. Therefore, in the summer of 1755, Braddock went to battle facing not winter-wearied, malnourished, exhausted Canadian militia, but fresh and well-fed French soldiers and French leadership well-informed of Braddock's intent.

Nonetheless, Braddock made astonishing progress towards Fort Duquesne after having set out from Alexandria. He had chosen to divide his forces so that one column was able to move significantly faster than the rest of the men. On the morning of July 9, Braddock and his reduced force crossed the Monongahela River just a few miles from Fort Duquesne. They had experienced no opposition while fording the river; Braddock was of the mind that the French had simply abandoned the fort.

They had not. Instead, a force of nearly 900 men had marched out to intercept Braddock's force. Though Braddock's reduced company was still superior in numbers, the French assault was nonetheless brutal, due in large part to the number of Indians among their ranks who fired upon them from the woods as the confused British troops attempted to advance along the road. After a three hour battle, Braddock was shot in the back, at which point the remaining British soldiers broke and ran. George Washington, who had volunteered to serve under Braddock as a civilian, was Braddock's only uninjured aide, even though he'd had two horses shot from underneath him and his clothes were riddled with bullet holes. Braddock died from his wounds as his company retreated. Upon reuniting with the rest of the men Braddock had left behind, the whole army fell back to Philadelphia. The French were still firmly in control of the Pennsylvania frontier.

Neither did the other campaigns of 1755 go as planned for the British. General William Shirley, who was meant to lead his troops upon Fort Niagara, faced large numbers of desertions after news of Braddock's defeat. Without the necessary men to embark on the Niagara, Shirley instead elected to winter his troops at Fort Oswego, planning an attempt to take the fort the following spring.

Yet Oswego was not adequately supplied to sustain them for the winter; by springtime the men were so malnourished and unhealthy, the campaign could not even begin. Moreover, the French governor Vaudreuil took advantage of the English troops' vulnerable position at Oswego, wreaking havoc with their supply lines throughout the summer of 1756. By the end of August, Oswego was under French control.

Major General William Johnson led the march to Fort Frederick on Lake Champlain but was foiled by Baron Dieskau, who had learned of the plan after Braddock's war chest had been captured at his defeat. Johnson's troops were surprised by the French force as Braddock's men had been, but Johnson's men were able to fall back to their fortified camp and then to return fire on Dieskau. The French then retreated to Fort Frederick, having suffered about the same number of casualties as the English. After this point, an attack on Fort Frederick was unrealistic, and Johnson instead ordered the construction of Fort William Henry and Fort Edward as a defense against the new French Fort Carillon on Lake George.

The only British success of 1755 was in Acadia, what is today known as Nova Scotia. Lieutenant Colonel Robert Monckton led a force out of Boston that succeeded in capturing Forts Beausejour and Gaspereau. These strongholds guarded the land route between the indomitable fortress of Louisbourg and Quebec, and the French surrendered them with surprisingly little resistance. While not as great a prize as Louisbourg herself, the victory was a significant one in that it resulted in the forced deportation of the largely Catholic, French-speaking Acadian population. Many of these refugees were put on boats to France or were dispersed throughout Louisiana. In their settlements around New Orleans, Acadians would come to be known by the now familiar term "Cajun."

After all that, 1755 was a great failure in terms of British goals. Their aim was to strike the French with force and thus avoid a full-scale war. The opposite happened. The English struck clumsily, handing Louis XV more than sufficient reason for a proper declaration of war, yet it was ultimately the course of events in Europe and elsewhere that led the French crown to open hostilities with England officially.

In King's George's War of 1743-1748, England had been closely allied with Austria, though the terms of the peace were more favorable to the former than to the latter. Moreover, conflict still roiled between Austria's empress Maria Theresa and the pugilistic Prussian ruler King Frederick. Disenchanted with Britain, Maria Theresa established diplomatic ties with France, while Britain's Hanoverian King George II instead sought an alliance with fellow German Frederick. In May of 1756, following the French capture of the British-held island of Minorca in the Mediterranean Sea, Great Britain and France each issued declarations of war against the other. Before the war's end, its battles would be fought over the entire globe. Known in Europe as the Seven Years War, this conflict became what Winston Churchill would later call "the first world war."

Chapter Four

Pitt Rising

"England has long been in labor, but at last she has brought forth a man."

—Frederick the Great, upon William Pitt's appointment as secretary of state, 1756

Historian Lawrence Henry Gipson referred to the period of 1753-1757 as "the years of defeat" for Great Britain in this global conflict. Forts and territory were lost; their Indian allies were faltering; their offensive efforts had failed. The French, meanwhile, were excelling on the battlefield but had suffered the loss of their military commander Baron Dieskau during the fighting at Fort Frederick. In 1756, both sides required a change in leadership. John Campbell, the fourth earl of Loudoun, became commander in chief of the British troops in North America, while Lieutenant General Louis-Joseph de Montcalm-Gozon was appointed supreme commander of the French forces.

It was Montcalm who presided over the siege and capture of Fort Oswego, the pivotal British stronghold on Lake Ontario. However, Montcalm only took command of the mission in July of 1756; the planning and execution of the siege had begun under the provincial Canadian governor Vaudreuil. These two men had vastly different viewpoints about the nature and purpose of war. Montcalm was thoroughly European in his approach; he felt that wars should be conducted according to agreed-upon standards and that one's enemies who behaved honorably should be treated with honor. Vaudreuil, who had grown up in the wilds of Louisiana, had adopted a less idealistic view. He knew the French needed Indian help to win the war, and he, therefore, had no intention of holding the Indians accountable to European standards of behavior. When Oswego fell, the Indians who had aided in its demise proceeded to kill many of the British wounded and to take the rest captive, as was their typical practice. Montcalm was horrified and expended a great deal of time and goods to redeem the captives the Indians had taken. This event opened a rift between Montcalm and Vaudreuil about the way in which the war should be conducted, and the two men were never able to come to an agreeable partnership on the matter.

On the British side, the fall of Oswego was evidence of disorganized leadership and the difficulty of maintaining unity among both British regular soldiers and the less-disciplined provincial militias. There were many regulations about the interactions between these two groups, the most galling being the subjection of the provincial soldiers and officers to the officers of the professional regiments. The first commander of the British forces in America was William Shirley, the previous governor of Massachusetts. He was not a trained soldier but a politician, and he put in place several measures intended to circumvent British regulations, to satisfy the demands of the provincial assemblies, and therefore to procure more provincial soldiers for the war effort. When Loudoun arrived that summer to replace Shirley, just as Montcalm was preparing to march on Oswego, he saw Shirley's measures as disordered and dangerous rather than expedient. Furthermore, it was Shirley who had left the troops at Fort Oswego that winter under-supplied and vulnerable to French raids. After its fall, Loudoun was sure to place the blame squarely on Shirley's shoulders, yet Loudoun did not have the support of the colonial assemblies as Shirley had. The British-American leadership in 1756 remained dangerously fractured.

These fractures were magnified across the Atlantic. With the declaration of war in Europe, King George II, who was also sovereign over the Hanover region of Germany, and his prime minister, the duke of Newcastle, were unsure how to proceed. France had taken Minorca and soon after the British lost their settlement in Calcutta, India, as well. Their Prussian ally Frederick had invaded Saxony and was asking for support on the continent. The news from North America was no better, where Indian raids on the colonial frontiers were seemingly endless. With the capture of Fort Oswego, British leadership had reached a point of crisis.

In that fateful moment, with Great Britain's empire in the balance, William Pitt the Elder declared, "I know that I can save England, and that no one else can." Pitt, however, was no favorite of King George II or of Newcastle. A member of the House of Commons, he was a champion of the middle class and a thorn in the side of the king, but he clearly had a plan to win the war and secure the peace, and the king needed him. He was appointed secretary of state in December of 1756, but after a public quarrel with George II, Pitt was dismissed in April 1757. In desperate need of the people's support and of Pitt's strategy, the king and Newcastle reinstated Pitt as secretary of state in June of 1757, with vast authority to conduct the war as he saw fit.

One of the first actions Pitt took was to recall Loudoun as commander in chief in North America and to replace him with General James Abercromby. Pitt also sent instructions to the colonial assemblies to raise as many provincial regiments as they could, promising that the crown would assume responsibility for payment of all expenses related to the war and ensuring that provincial officers would have equal rank as officers of the regular army, subject only to regular officers of their own rank or higher.

Though these measures were costly for Britain, they allowed the colonies to assert the importance of their role in winning North America. Almost immediately, the colonies raised the money, men, and supplies necessary for the war effort.

In another shrewd move, Pitt found a way to take advantage of Frederick's war on the continent. Rather than merely being a drain on Britain's resources, Prussia's incursions into Austria served as an excellent distraction. France was highly vested in its supremacy in Europe, and its alliance with Austria required giving attention to these continental land battles. Canada - which now seemed relatively secure, from France's point of view - would become the less urgent theater of war. Pitt invested just enough of Britain's military power in Europe to distract France from what Britain considered to be the real prize: North America.

France's position in North America was still the stronger one, and Pitt knew that small skirmishes in the frontiers of the Ohio Valley would never be decisive. If a lasting wound were to be inflicted, it must be in the very heart of New France. Pitt was resolved; they must take Quebec. Yet how to proceed? From the sea, Quebec could be reached via the St. Lawrence River, but not without first taking the stronghold at Louisbourg. From land, Quebec was guarded by Forts Carillon (the British called it by its Indian name, Ticonderoga) and Frederick. Pitt determined to attempt both.

Another goal of strategic and symbolic importance was the French garrison Fort Duquesne. Since Braddock's defeat, Fort Duquesne had served as a base from which Ohio Indians could raid the English frontiers at will, and the Pennsylvania and Virginia settlements had suffered greatly. The job of removing the French and Indian presence once and for all from that stronghold fell to Brigadier General John Forbes. If this could be accomplished, the line of French forts across the Ohio Valley would be substantially weakened.

The final piece of Pitt's plan was to prevent France from sending reinforcements to North America by means of naval supremacy. Britain's superior navy was to concentrate its efforts in patrolling French ports both on the Atlantic and along the English Channel. Yet before Pitt would see victory with his proposed plan to capture North America from France, his nation was to suffer two more disastrous losses. The "years of defeat" were not yet over.

Chapter Five

The Montcalm Before the Storm

"Christian, behold!... The arm of God prevailed, the victor of this cross."

—General Montcalm, upon his surprising victory at Fort Carillon, July 8, 1758

Before Pitt could begin execution of his strategy to take Quebec by way of Louisbourg, Lord Loudoun had already made an attempt, which was no more successful than any other British campaign of 1757. Loudoun had gotten as far as Halifax on Nova Scotia before determining that he was too outnumbered, retreating to Boston for the winter.

In Loudoun's absence, the number of soldiers on the New York frontier was markedly low. Lieutenant-General Montcalm moved his men south from Quebec to take advantage of their depleted defenses. His goal was to take Fort William Henry, located at the southern end of Lake George. Governor Vaudreuil had tried unsuccessfully to take the fort in March of that year, and Montcalm did not intend to fail in the same endeavor, bringing together a company of 8,000 French and Canadian soldiers to join in the effort. There were also thousands of Indians in their ranks, the presence of which greatly displeased Montcalm after his experience at Fort Oswego, but Vaudreuil welcomed their aid precisely because of incidents like Oswego; a strong Indian presence would, he knew, terrify the enemy.

With Loudoun and his second-in-command, Major General James Abercromby, away on the fruitless Louisbourg expedition, the British third in command was Brigadier General Daniel Webb. As scouts began reporting the movement of French and Indian forces in the area, Webb did little to bolster the defenses at Fort William Henry, sending a detachment of only 200 men, though he had as many as 3,500 men at his disposal. It is unclear whether Webb intended to draw the French further south to his post at Fort Edward, or whether he acted from sheer incompetence; either way, the 2,000 men at Fort William Henry were severely outnumbered, and there was little to be done in anticipation of the siege.

It began on August 3, 1757, and ended on August 9. Colonel George Munro, the commanding officer at Fort William Henry, had fought nobly in spite of receiving a message from Webb that no relief force was coming. When Montcalm offered him an honorable surrender, Munro accepted. According to the terms, Munro and his men promised they would not engage in battle for 18 months. In return, they would be allowed to march unhindered to Fort Edward and to maintain their arms and personal effects. The battle had been conducted by gentlemen, and the surrender was meant to be so as well.

Montcalm's worst fears about his Indian allies were realized on the morning of August 10. As the British troops began their departure for Fort Edward, they were mercilessly attacked by the Indians who had aided the French in their defeat. Montcalm had, of course, explained to them that by the terms of the surrender, there was to be no plundering of loot and no taking of captives, but these were the very prizes for which the Indians had fought. They had no precedent for "honorable" European-style warfare. To the contrary, they saw the whole affair as thoroughly dishonorable, since they were being denied the spoils of war they had been promised, and so the Indians viciously took what they believed was theirs. Hundreds of British soldiers were killed, wounded, or taken captive. The event came to be known as "the massacre of Fort William Henry."

Montcalm was mortified and again tried desperately to ransom prisoners that had been carried away, but the damage had been done, with devastating effect. The colonists accused Montcalm of premeditating the attack, and the British refused to offer honorable surrender to the French for the remainder of the war. Montcalm's Indian allies, now satisfied with their plunder, were abandoning the French, most of them never to return. Without the aid of Indian scouts and warriors, the French were uneasy about continuing the campaign to Fort Edward and Albany. Instead, they destroyed the remains of Fort William Henry and returned to Canada. The rift between Vaudreuil and Montcalm became a chasm, as each openly blamed the fiasco on the other.

Montcalm's reputation was stained, but he was by no means finished in North America, and he would, in fact, become a pivotal player in another important victory over the British. The Battle of Fort Carillon was the most improbable of victories, given that the French were desperately short of both men and provisions. Despite France's successes in the war, their North American forces were suffering from the success of the English fleet's blockade of French supply ships. France needed to strike a decisive blow to end the conflict quickly.

Fort Carillon, like Forts William Henry and Edward, had been hastily constructed after the fighting at Fort Frederick in 1755 had failed to produce a victor. Positioned to the south of Lake Champlain, it would provide a suitable point of departure for a march on Fort Edward. The French planned from there to take the key city of Albany. Yet when Montcalm arrived at Fort Carillon in the summer of 1758, he found it badly undermanned and dangerously low on provisions. Having learned of a great British force being assembled near Albany, Governor Vaudreuil sent

Brigadier General Francois Gaston de Levis with 3,000 men to come to Montcalm's aid.

The number was still paltry compared to the numbers of British troops. Pitt's new regulations regarding the recruitment of colonial soldiers, along with the patriotic fervor inspired by the Fort William Henry massacre, had swollen the regiments to the point that General Abercromby commanded a force of nearly 16,000 men. On July 5, they set out from their headquarters at Lake George with 16 heavy cannon and 8,000 rounds of ammunition. When the army set out to cross Lake George, they formed four columns stretching for seven miles, covering the breadth of the lake. Montcalm was severely outmanned and outgunned.

Montcalm was granted an extra day of preparation due to a tragedy that befell Abercromby's second in command, George Augustus, viscount Howe. When Pitt could not dissuade King George II from replacing Lord Loudoun with Abercromby as commander in chief in America, Pitt hand-picked Howe to be Abercromby's deputy. In Howe, Pitt had chosen an able man whom the soldiers trusted and admired. Howe was once commanded with overseeing Major Roger Roberts and his famous rangers, a group that had grown famous for their bravery and stealth, yet the rangers were not regular soldiers; they used unconventional tactics and were notoriously undisciplined. When Howe was charged with instructing the rangers in proper military conduct, he instead took the opportunity to learn Rogers' tactics and to implement some of them among the regular soldiers. With methods like these, Howe inspired unity among the troops and was greatly loved by them.

Howe and Rogers, along with Lieutenant Colonel Thomas Gage, were among the first of Abercromby's troops to land on the northern side of Lake George on July 6. They led the advance units through the forest towards Fort Carillon, but Howe's unit met members of the French advance guard also rushing north to the fort. They were no match for the elite British units, but in the skirmish, Howe was shot in the chest and died almost instantly. The effect of his death was profound; Abercromby required an entire day to recover himself.

The delay allowed Montcalm time to plan a defense. He instructed his men to dig a line of trenches on the north side of the fort. They then spent the day felling trees, which they used to create a barrier of sharp and tangled branches below the trenches. This barrier, called an abatis, was intended to slow the attackers' movement up the hill towards the fort and had the added benefit of making anyone caught in it an easy target from above. Still, Montcalm did not believe the barrier would hold. He knew the fort was exposed at its sides and could easily be destroyed by heavy artillery fire from the surrounding hills.

But the grieving and bewildered Abercromby elected not to wait until the artillery - the cannon his men had labored to transport across the lake - could be hauled into place. Instead, relying solely on the assessment of a junior officer, Abercromby ordered the ranks into position for a frontal assault straight through Montcalm's abatis.

The result was a crushing defeat for Abercromby's army. The British lines moved bravely forward only to be broken by the fallen trees and then destroyed by the French assault from the trenches. By nightfall, the British had suffered nearly 2,000 casualties; the French, less than 400. Montcalm expected their attackers to charge the following morning again, and Abercromby intended to, yet Abercromby's order to pull back three miles confused the soldiers, who feared an impending attack by the French. In a panic, they ran for the boats and rowed for their lives back across Lake George.

Having secured Fort Carillon from the superior British forces, Montcalm was quick to use the prestige gained in battle to his advantage. He wrote to the king asking for unlimited authority to wage the war, effectively seeking to have Vaudreuil excluded from leadership. The French crown agreed, ensuring that Vaudreuil's preferred method of reliance upon Indian allies to win battles would end. Montcalm was then free to run campaigns as he saw fit, in a professional manner, and without having to manage unpredictable Indian warriors. For Montcalm, this was a political victory almost as great as his military victory.

By the time Montcalm received news of the king's decision, the balance of power in North America had shifted drastically. Though Fort Carillon was indeed a crushing blow to the British army, it was not the permanent one that Montcalm had hoped it would be. By April of 1759, Louis XV had given Montcalm the sole authority to carry out a war that he would not be able to win.

Chapter Six

Fortresses Fall

"What good is Louisbourg?"

—an unnamed French priest, upon witnessing the Acadian
deportation of 1758

Louisbourg had long been a symbol of French power in the New World. Situated at the mouth of the Saint Lawrence River, the fortified town had been established as a cod fishing outpost but quickly grew into one of the busiest ports in North America. Its position of strength protected supply lines all the way down the Saint Lawrence to Lake Ontario and beyond, but despite its reputation as an "impregnable fortress," Louisbourg was home to nearly as many civilians as soldiers. In the summer of 1758, Governor Augustin de Drucour was in command of 3,500 French soldiers at Louisbourg.

Pitt's choice to lead the siege of Louisbourg was Major General Jeffrey Amherst, with Brigadier General James Wolfe as second in command. Also central to Pitt's strategy was the presence of Admiral Edward Boscawen, who would command the English fleet during the attack. All assembled at Halifax and then embarked for Louisbourg on May 28, 1758, with some 13,000 men in a fleet of 150 ships.

By far, the most difficult and dangerous aspect of the coming siege was the landing of the troops along the rocky coast. On the morning of June 8, the fleet was poised off Gabarus Bay just south of Louisbourg. Wolfe had been chosen to lead the main landing force at Kennington Cove toward the western end of the bay, while two other divisions were to land further east. The bay itself was heavily defended by French forces; Drucour, like Montcalm at Fort Carillon, had entrenched his men behind a deep abatis all along the bay, awaiting the enemy's arrival. Wolfe, who had been chosen to lead the landing expedition, had little choice about where to land; indeed there was very nearly no choice at all. Along with the thunder of French artillery and musket fire round about them, the waves were so fierce that several of the landing boats were capsized. There appeared no safe place to go ashore. At the last minute, Wolfe spotted three of his boats making for a small alcove that was sufficiently sheltered from both the waves and the French defenses. Wolfe directed his men to follow them, and the landing was made.

Once ashore, Wolfe immediately organized the men with him into formation to face the entrenched French force. Wolfe himself had no bayonet, leading them into battle carrying only a walking stick, yet they prevailed; as the French troops closest to Wolfe were furthest from Louisbourg, they feared being cut off from their command and soon abandoned their defenses. In the meantime, the remainder of Amherst's army was coming ashore at Kennington Cove instead of the more easterly locations, but the French defensive force was spread all across the bay waiting for an enemy arrival that had already come. Soon they too were retreating back to Louisbourg. By the following morning, the city was surrounded. Boscawen had by that time trapped the few French naval ships in the Louisbourg harbor. Amherst now had only to wait.

Conditions inside Louisbourg were dire. The town was already short of food. Only one supply ship had provided its people with any relief throughout the entire winter of 1758. The British noted that the French soldiers they encountered were unwell and clearly hungry. Drucour was no fool; he knew that Louisbourg would eventually fall to the British. However, he hoped to draw out the siege as long as possible as a means of preserving Quebec. If the British were occupied with Louisbourg for the remainder of the summer, there would be little time to pursue an assault on Quebec before the weather turned, yet by mid-July it was obvious he could not withstand much longer. The French fleet had been decimated; thanks to Admiral Boscawen on July 25, it was annihilated as their two remaining ships were lost - one taken by Boscawen, the other burned. On July 26, Drucour asked Amherst for the terms of surrender. Once again, Louisbourg was in the hands of the British, and French control of the Saint Lawrence River was over.

Amherst's first priority as victor was to remove the remaining Acadian population in Nova Scotia. In the end, Louisbourg could not protect them.

Having Louisbourg in hand put Pitt in sight of his goal to take Quebec, but it did not assure him of victory. Abercromby's failure at Fort Carillon was a profound disappointment and left the General unsure of what course to pursue next. The answer was provided for him by the ambitious and daring Captain John Bradstreet, who knew exactly what to do.

Bradstreet had long seen the strategic importance of Fort Frontenac, located at the confluence of the Saint Lawrence with Lake Ontario. Frontenac was the commercial gateway of New France. All goods moving west and east passed through it, with much of its resources being stored outside the walls. Frontenac was critical for supplying other forts in the region, notably Forts Niagara and Duquesne; to weaken it was to weaken defenses throughout New France, and since Frontenac had not sustained attack in over 80 years, it was militarily neglected. Bradstreet wasted no time in besieging the fort, which was commanded by Major Pierre-Jacques Payen de Noyan. He marched up the Mohawk

River in August of 1758 and arrived at Frontenac before the end of the month.

Noyan had been warned by Indian scouts about Bradstreet's advance and wrote to Vaudreuil to send reinforcements; at the time there were about 110 men at the fort, plus women and children. Vaudreuil complied, but the troops could never have arrived in time. Bradstreet laid siege to Frontenac on August 26. Before two full days had passed, Frontenac was his. Fueled by his victory, Bradstreet ordered his men to take all the plunder they could - and this was substantial, given Frontenac's stores. On a whim and out of desperation, Abercromby had allowed Bradstreet to strike a critical blow against New France's already suffering strongholds. Fueled by his victory, Bradstreet went on to recover Fort Oswego, lost three years earlier, before returning to Abercromby. Bradstreet then pressed Abercromby to allow him to continue the campaign against Fort Niagara, but Abercromby inexplicably refused.

For much of the war, France had benefited enormously from its Indian alliances. Several French victories were owed in large part to the Indian warriors of the Ohio Valley tribes who were almost all loyal to France. Members of these tribes - among them Delaware, Shawnee, and Mingo - were responsible for the relentless raids on English settlements in the Pennsylvania and Virginia frontiers, the defense of which kept men like George Washington busy for the remainder of the war. On the other hand, England's main alliance, by means of the historic Covenant Chain, was with the Iroquois League. Yet despite the many gifts they had received at the Albany Conference in 1754, the league's main contribution to Britain's war effort was their continued neutrality rather than their active partnership. All this was about to change through the leadership of John Forbes in the campaign to capture Fort Duquesne.

Rather than take the same road built by Washington and marched upon by the ill-fated Braddock, Forbes undertook a prolonged march towards Fort Duquesne in late July straight through the Pennsylvania wilderness. The approach was slow and expensive but allowed the army greater stability. By October they had come within 40 miles of Fort Duquesne.

Forbes paused in October to hold a conference with several representatives of the Delaware and Shawnee tribes as well as the Iroquois League. One key Indian leader, Teedyuscung of the eastern Delaware, who had enacted promises of reserved lands from the Pennsylvania government the year before, used his influence to bring western Delaware and Shawnee groups to the table. Meeting in Easton, Pennsylvania, the British and Indian representatives signed the Treaty of Easton, which maintained independence for the Delaware and Shawnee and freedom from Iroquois oversight in local matters while still returning much of the western Pennsylvania lands to Iroquois control. In return, the Delaware and Shawnee tribes agreed they would no longer defend the French at Fort Duquesne. The treaty was signed on October 25, 1758. Soon after, the Indians who had so long remained with the French at Fort Duquesne were gone.

When the French learned of the treaty and the loss of their Indian allies, they panicked. Having lost their supply line by way of Fort Frontenac, they could not withstand a winter siege. On November 25, Forbes' army heard explosions and scouts reported smoke rising from the Fort. The French had destroyed Fort Duquesne and abandoned it. The next day, Forbes and his men took control of the forks of the Ohio. The new stronghold was named Fort Pitt; the settlement that grew up around it: Pittsburgh.

Chapter Seven

From the Plains of Abraham to Peace

"The Romans were three hundred years in conquering the world. We subdued the globe in three campaigns."

—Horace Walpole, 1762

After another winter with little provisions, the French resolve on the frontier had finally been broken. During the campaigns of 1759, French forts fell with little resistance and with startling speed. Fort Carillon (now Fort Ticonderoga) was captured in June. Fort Frederick (now Crown Point) and Fort Niagara were surrendered in July. By the end of the summer, the only fort in the western frontier remaining under French control was Fort Pontchartrain near Detroit. The one remaining piece of Pitt's plan to win North America that remained was to take Quebec. The British blockade on French ships had continued all winter, but some supply ships had managed to slip through, preserving the city and allowing Montcalm to mount a reasonable defense.

Pitt had named Amherst commander in chief following Abercromby's defeat and promoted Wolfe to Major General. Wolfe would take the lead in advancing on Quebec while Vice-Admiral Charles Saunders was to lead the British fleet up the Saint Lawrence. Beginning on June 26, British troops occupied the Island of Orleans in the river just opposite Quebec. The bombardment began in mid-July, but Montcalm was determined not to panic. He operated his defense masterfully, unnerving the hot-tempered Wolfe, who was unable to wear down Montcalm's patience and fortitude. In July, the British were repelled by the French at Montmorency Falls, downriver from Quebec.

Wolfe was unwell in the fall of 1759, not merely with anxiety over his current inability to break Quebec's defenses but also physically as he was plagued with fever and pain. All attempts to gain the advantage in Quebec failed. The month of August passed anxiously, as Wolfe waited for news from General Amherst. He was delighted to hear of the British capture of Forts Ticonderoga, Crown Point, and Niagara, yet he hoped in vain that Amherst might then come from the south via the land route Pitt had originally designed. Wolfe was unsure how to proceed, and while taking opiates to relieve his chronic pain, he did not trust his own wisdom but turned to that of his brigadier generals. To a man, Wolfe's deputies sanctioned taking the battle to Quebec's south shore in order to cut Montcalm off from communication with Montreal. During the first week of September, the British forces began movement of men and supplies upriver.

Montcalm imagined that the British activities upriver from Quebec were merely a diversion. He remained at camp on the Beauport shoals downriver from Quebec until September 12. That evening, Wolfe dispatched Admiral Saunders to the river beside Montcalm's camp where he engaged in just such a diversion as Montcalm was hoping to avoid. Saunders made a great show of lowering boats and bombing the French position, while Wolfe was several miles to the south preparing to come on shore.

Wolfe had chosen his landing place secretly, consulting no one, not even his brigadier generals. They were most perturbed at having been left out of his deliberations, but Wolfe remained stubbornly cryptic about his plans, perhaps because the place he had chosen was fantastically inaccessible. Anse au Foulon was a small cove wide enough to handle the debarkation of his troops, but once they were ashore, they would then have to ascend an 180-foot bluff before reaching a broad plateau known as the Plains of Abraham leading straight to Quebec. The success of such an attempt was altogether unlikely; perhaps the better, then, that Wolfe did not share his plans. By the time his brigadiers realized what was happening, the assault had begun. There was a small French force at the top of the bluff which Wolfe's men dispatched with ease. Wolfe then began positioning his men in the pre-dawn hours of September 13 and waited for sunrise.

Montcalm had left this side of Quebec largely unfortified, believing that the bluffs were too insurmountable an obstacle for an enemy landing. Montcalm was caught completely by surprise. While Quebec slept, Wolfe had amassed a force of 4,800 troops on the wide plains leading to the vulnerable city.

By 10:00 that morning, Montcalm had positioned a comparable force of 4,500 on the field opposite Wolfe's men and gave the order to charge. His troops were a mix of French regular soldiers and untrained Canadian militiamen; as they advanced towards the British line, they moved with no recognizable order and fired intermittently. The British watched as the French line became increasingly confused. Then, on order, they began to level the French with coordinated musket fire. Soon the French lines broke down altogether; as they retreated, Wolfe ordered a bayonet charge, chasing them back to the city walls.

The battle lasted less than 15 minutes. Wolfe sustained multiple wounds and perished on the field, shot through the chest. Montcalm was wounded in the stomach and died the following morning. The British command fell to Lord George Townshend, who hastily organized the remaining troops to face the newly arrived reinforcements from Montcalm's aid Louis-Antoine de Bougainville. Just as Bougainville appeared to ride to Montcalm's rescue, he hesitated at the sight of them. Quebec was lost. The surrender was signed on September 18, and the French, now led by General Francois-Gaston de Levis, retreated to Jacques-Cartier in the Montreal district.

James Murray, Wolfe's junior brigadier general, remained to oversee the British occupation of Quebec, and the task was arduous. For one thing, Quebec remained poorly supplied, so the British were no better off in the winter of 1760 than the French had been in 1759. Diseases, especially dysentery and scurvy, were rampant, and funerals were held daily. Added to this, Murray bore the strain of anticipating the French assault he was sure would come in the spring; of the 7,000 men who entered Quebec with him the previous fall, only about 3,000 were alive and fit for duty by winter's end.

At the end of April, Murray met Levis in battle, once again on the Plains of Abraham, but this time the British fared only slightly better than the French had the previous autumn. After the costly encounter, Murray and his men were besieged within the walls of Quebec. Murray's only hope was the much-anticipated arrival of the British navy. On May 9, 1760, the first ship to appear on the horizon of the Saint Lawrence River after a long, harsh winter was the frigate Lowestoft, the British relief ship Murray had longed to see. By May 16, the siege was over, and the French had been once again driven from Quebec.

All of Pitt's North American objectives had been achieved by the summer of 1760. The only remaining French holding in North America was the island of Montreal and its surrounding area. Amherst dispatched both land and sea forces to converge upon them from three directions: Murray would sail upriver from Quebec, Brigadier-General William Haviland would march north from Crown Point on Lake Champlain, and Amherst himself would lead a force down the Saint Lawrence from Fort Oswego in the west. There would be nowhere left for Levis to go.

To his credit, Levis and his men resisted bravely, but in addition to their vastly outnumbered ranks, there was another factor of the battle operating against them. The surrounding Indian tribes, previously dependable French allies, had made peace with Britain. Amherst had wisely taken advantage of the long-standing Covenant Chain alliance and enlisted Iroquois aid as the British moved towards Montreal. About 700 Iroquois warriors traveled with Amherst's army; their presence was a powerful means of persuading the local Mohawk Indians not to hinder their movement against France, and in many cases to aid it. By early September, Levis was entirely bereft of Indian allies, and he retreated to Montreal to await Amherst's arrival.

Governor Vaudreuil signed the articles of surrender on September 8, 1760, and the next day the flag of Great Britain was raised over Montreal. One week later Major Rogers removed the last French flag in the west, raising the Union Jack over Fort Detroit. Britain now held sway over the Ohio Valley and Canada; William Pitt had saved England.

Though the war in America was won, in Europe, it wore on. In 1760, Frederick the Great had secured Hanover from France - the only real concern of King George II, and indeed of Pitt as well - but his army languished in a stalemate against the French and Austrian forces. This circumstance was fine with Pitt as long as he was free to continue securing Britain's imperial interests elsewhere. In 1761, British commander Robert Clive and Colonel Eyre Coote regained Calcutta, severely curtailing French influence in India. Britain also wreaked havoc with French holdings in the Caribbean, seeking to disrupt their trade in rum, sugar, and slaves. The island of Guadalupe fell, then Dominique, Martinique, and the rest of the French Antilles. Spain, now under the leadership of their new king Charles III (a distant cousin to Louis XV), belatedly entered the war on the side of the French in 1762, and the British fleet in the

Caribbean wasted no time in turning its guns on Cuba. Havana fell on August 13. Then, in October, Lieutenant Colonel William Draper seized the Spanish stronghold of Manila in the Philippines. The British people were exultant; their nation held dominion wherever she pleased.

In the midst of what were undoubtedly the years of victory for Great Britain, the man who had done so much to secure that victory resigned his office. King George II, who had forged a reluctant partnership with Pitt, died in October 1760, to be succeeded by his grandson George III. The new king was supremely interested in ending the war as quickly as possible and was, therefore, eager to remove Pitt from office. Once Charles III came to power in Spain and began making political overtures toward France, Pitt saw that war with Spain was inevitable and urged the king to declare war preemptively. When George III repeatedly refused, Pitt countered by threatening resignation. But Parliament was not willing to back Pitt in his gamble, and George III called his bluff. On October 5, 1761, Pitt tendered his resignation.

King George III navigated the war to its end in 1762. The Treaty of Paris was ratified on February 10, 1763, and it handed all French claims in North America east of the Mississippi (except New Orleans) to Great Britain. England also received back the island of Minorca, while France regained almost all their islands in the Caribbean. Spain ceded Florida to Britain but regained Cuba. France returned the German territories they had acquired to their respective princes but was granted fishing rights off two small islands in the Gulf of Saint Lawrence. For their part, Prussia and Austria signed a separate peace treaty restoring both of their kingdoms to their former boundaries before hostilities began. The long war was over.

The terms of peace were much to the liking of King George III but were vastly different from what Pitt would have chosen. Not only was the king eager to end the war, but he was also similarly uneager to administer all of the lands that Great Britain had conquered. He feared to commit his empire to more than she could reasonably manage. Though his caution may have been wise, it was not popular. Many Britons, including Pitt, felt that the terms of peace fell far short of what the long war had accomplished. Pitt remarked, "The peace was insecure, because it restored the enemy to her former greatness. The peace was inadequate, because the places gained were no equivalent for the places surrendered." His feelings would be borne out in less than a generation's time, as Britain faced rebellion within the bounds of the empire, leading ultimately to another colonial war, the war for American Independence.

Conclusion

In the aftermath of the French and Indian War, General Amherst had been left with the formidable task of administering the North American territories. Facing a severe lack of funds, Amherst devised a series of ways to cut expenses, most notably by suspending the long-held practice of gift-giving to Indian tribes. He also restricted trade among the Indians, particularly that of rum. Amherst placed these measures into effect at a time when many tribes were feeling ever more threatened by the apparent permanence of British forts and settlements in the Ohio Valley. There were drastic consequences. A series of Indian insurrections in the spring of 1763 ultimately amounted to a pan-Indian revolt, the most brutal and successful of any Indian uprising in North America. While American colonial governments struggled to deal with the crisis, George III issued the Proclamation of 1763 in October as a means of reaffirming the provisions of the Treaty of Easton and assuring the Indians that formal settlement west of the Appalachian Mountains was strictly prohibited. The tribes were satisfied, and the insurrection was ended, but the crises in the American colonies were far from over.

In 1757, Pitt had engendered colonial support for the war by removing heavy-handed leaders who were openly disrespectful of the colonial legislatures and militias. He also acknowledged their cooperation as central to the war effort by committing imperial funds to support colonial militias; the crown had promised to take on the expense necessary to pay, arm, clothe, feed, and quarter them. Whether Pitt truly saw the colonies as partners or was merely exercising political shrewdness to achieve his desired result is inconsequential. The colonists considered themselves to be the equals of any subject of the empire, and they would not easily forfeit that status.

However, the debts Britain incurred during the war demanded to be paid. Therefore the crown began to levy a series of taxes exclusive to the colonies. To the Loyalist British mind, the taxes were fair because the war had been fought on behalf of the colonists, to defend them against the French and Indian threat. Why shouldn't they carry the majority – if not all – of the subsequent tax burden? The taxes imposed in the 1760s were indeed burdensome during the postwar recession, but the colonists objected on ideological as well as economic grounds. To the American mind, the issue was not taxation but consent. The colonists believed they had a right to consent to the taxes placed upon them; this consent could easily be achieved by electing colonial representatives to Parliament. Without Parliamentary representation, they would be little more than slaves.

This suggestion was wholly disagreeable to George III and to the members of Parliament. To bow to demands such as these would be to afford these imperial subjects a dangerous level of power. The empire could only operate with all its members functioning in their proper and appointed roles, and Parliamentary representation was beyond the bounds of the colonists' imperial purpose. They feared it would lead to dangerous fissures in the unity of the constitutional monarchy.

Unfortunately, Pitt had already introduced these fissures by means of his wartime colonial policies. The responsibility for the resulting American Revolution is of course not to be placed solely on Pitt's shoulders, though. One of the reasons for its success lay in the Treaty of Paris, which gave back to France much of what it had lost in the Seven Years' War. Because France was not broken by the Treaty, it lived to fight another day, and one of the fights it undertook was the cause of American Independence. The United

States of America, liberated from the British Empire and allied with France, would constitute a serious blow to British power. The prospect appealed to France so much that they began covertly sending supplies to the Americans as early as 1775 and became the first nation to recognize the fledgling United States in 1778.

The world we inhabit is due in large part to the outcome of the French and Indian War. Within two years of its inception, the battle for North America sparked the Seven Years' War in Europe. Within two years of its conclusion, it produced not only unstable Indian relations and the nascent American independence movement. When Great Britain emerged the victor of this global contest, their power seemed limitless, yet the French and Indian War and its aftermath imparts a great lesson to us: that power is often an illusion, and that when wielded carelessly it will sow the seeds of its own undoing.

Made in the USA
Monee, IL
06 August 2021